Hydroponics: A Complete DIY Guide For Gardening Using Simple Steps

Hydroponics Builders Guide For Beginners And Intermediate Gardeners

Allen Dunn

© 2012 by **Allen Dunn**

ISBN-13: 978-1480236141
ISBN-10: 1480236144

College of the Ouachitas

First Printing, 2012

Printed in the United States of America

Disclaimer

This publication is intended to provide helpful and informative material. It is not intended to diagnose, treat, cure, or prevent any health problem or condition, nor is intended to replace the advice of a physician. No action should be taken solely on the contents of this book. Always consult your physician or qualified health-care professional on any matters regarding your health and before adopting any suggestions in this book or drawing inferences from it.

The author and publisher specifically disclaim all responsibility for any liability, loss or risk, personal or otherwise, which is incurred as a consequence, directly or indirectly, from the use or application of any contents of this book.

Any and all product names referenced within this book are the trademarks of their respective owners. None of these owners have sponsored, authorized, endorsed, or approved this book.

Always read all information provided by the manufacturers' product labels before using their products. The author and publisher are not responsible for claims made by manufacturers.

The statements made in this book have not been evaluated by the Food and Drug Administration.

Hydroponics: A Complete DIY Guide For Gardening Using Simple Steps

Hydroponics Builders Guide For Beginners And Intermediate Gardeners

Table of Contents

Chapter 1 – What is Hydroponic Gardening?

A simple definition of hydroponics is cultivating plants with water and nutrients but no soil. Water has to be transported to the root system of the plant. This system can directly hang in the solution of the nutrient, get misted with it or may be fenced in a trough or container that is packed with substrate (a soil substitute). There may be a lot of different kinds of materials in the substrate like sand, perlite, wood chips, sawdust, Rockwool or pebbles. Substrate should offer adequate capacity to hold water and still be absorbent for the exchange of gas. The roots of the plant grow in the substrate to make the plant secured within the trough or container.

Several techniques exist for delivering water to where the plant roots are. Each plant that is grown in a container is provided with a water emitter that is from an irrigation drip system. Nutrient film method system is one way that water can be transported through the row of plants in a trough. Another way is to water from beneath by filling up the whole tray with water, then draining the excess water. This is referred to as ebb and flow irrigation. Generally, water is recycled through this system as well as within the nutrient film technique. Recycling for the systems involving drip irrigation is harder and necessitates added equipment like equipment for adjusting and monitoring fertilizer and also a water sterilizer.

The hydroponic methods are further grouped as open (nutrient solution is not reusable after being delivered to root of plants) and closed (excess solution can be recovered, refilled and also recycled). Combined with greenhouses, this system is capital-intensive and high technology. In addition, it is highly productive, conserves land and water, and also protects the environment. However, for the majority of people, hydroponic culture calls for only basic skill in agriculture. As managing the root and aerial environment has become a great concern in agricultural systems such as these, production occurs within enclosures that are designed to regulate root temperatures, air, water, light, adverse climate and plant nutrition.

There are several kinds of hydroponic or controlled environment systems. Every component of CEA (controlled environment agriculture) is equally relevant, whether it is environmental control, growing system or structural design. Often importance is only placed on one or maybe two of the important components, and the system becomes unsuccessful because of the lack of attention that is given to other components.

Chapter 2 - How To Set Up Your Own Hydroponic Garden

Preparation of Starter Cubes

An easy method of starting cuttings or seeds is starter cubes. They are widely used in soil gardening as well as hydroponic cultivation. The starter cubes are produced out of a material that is inert; the only thing they provide for the plant and the roots is support. Some water is retained in the material but the only time it supplies nutrient is if nutrient is dissolved in the water before soaking. Starter cubes include Sure To Grow, Rockwool, Rapid Rooters, peat pots and Oasis cubes. Rapid Rooters have been considered to be the best for many years. This is because they are bio degradable, pH neutral, organic and they have a great oxygen : moisture ratio.

The peat pots are not as popular among gardeners anymore as

they tend to hold excess water and have the ability to drown seeds and seedlings. There is a more recent product available that is produced from coconut husks. It acts and looks like the regular Jiffy or peat pots but its performance is outstanding in comparison. The other ones mentioned all hold water suitably but also maintained adequate air to make the medium remain not too wet.

The preparation of starter cubes is different for each type of starter cube that you use. The Rapid Rooters are available as ready to used. Peat pot and Oasis cubes require presoaking with water of a particular adjustment. The cubes only require saturation followed by draining. They are now ready for use. Other starter cubes such as Rockwool also require presoaking because the pH is high. The cubes require soaking for half hour or so before draining and are then ready to be used.

When your starter cubes are ready, it is now time to plant the cuttings or seeds. Majority of starter cubes are available with the holes manufactured in them. You can use a bamboo skewer or something with a clean tip if your starter cube does not have a hole. Make a hole at the top that is about a quarter to half inch deep. Put cuttings or seeds in the hole; cover gently by lightly packing a little of the cube material that surrounds the hole on top of the seed or against the cutting stem.

Seed cubes must remain moist (not wet) and at no time allowed to remain in water. Light is required only after sprouting. For cuttings, light is required immediately for 18 to 24 hours. When seedlings come out of the cube is when they require nutrient. When they emerge, you may begin to give them a watered down nutrient solution having ¼ - ½ strength. For cuttings, pH adjusted water should be used to water them for the initial three days only, after which a bloom nutrient (¼ strength) is used until the roots come out of the cube.

Preparation of Nutrient Solution

Dissolved hydroponic fertilizer and water is what makes up the nutrient solution. For preparing this solution, begin with water of good quality like reverse osmosis (RO), well, distilled or spring and then combine it with the fertilizer using the ratio that the manufacturer provides. As it is so important, the pH of the nutrient solution should be measured and adjusted using liquid adjusters.

For every growing medium, the general rule in this case is that the pH should be set between 5.5 and 6 apart from Rockwool that requires pH 5.5. The young plants require a mixed nutrient solution with ¼ - ½ of the complete strength recommended by the manufacturer of the fertilizer. Nutrient solution of full strength can be applied when the plants have matured to two weeks old.

Transplanting the Seedlings

When roots are growing out of the seedlings in starter cubes, the plants can be transplanted. It simply requires putting the plant and the starter cube in or on the top of a medium that is constantly growing. This medium may be a type of growing hydroponic medium or even soil.

Two kinds of basic hydroponics systems exist and these are active and passive. You will learn here how the simple hydroponic arrangements should be set up and also which mediums are best suited to each of them.

For making an active, simple, one plant hydroponic system the materials listed below are required:

- 1-gallon pot for planting with holes for drainage
- 1-gallon bucket with no holes for drainage (utilized for reservoir of nutrient solution)
- 1 aquarium pump for water (small, for pumping nutrient solution to plant)
- 1 sm bag of pea gravel, perlite or vermiculite; sufficient for filling pot)
- 1 sm table with hole in top; large so that the planting pot can be placed in it without it falling right through
- 2 sm plasic tubes; suitably long to stretch from nutrient solution to water pump as well as from water pump to planting pot
- 2 board clothes pin for attaching plastic tubes to the container tops
- Timer (on/off) for attaching water pump to regulate the water going to the plant

How to Setup

Put the planting container in the hole in the table tophole. Fill pot with selected medium, to about 1-2 inches from the container top. Place the 2-gallon bucket right under the holes of the growing container to catch the water draining out of the pot. Put the water pump beside the reservoir on the floor.

Attach a plastic tube to the pump water intake and put other end in the reservoir. Ensure that the tube end is positioned at the bottom of the reservoir bucket and not positioned too close to the planting container bottom, preventing the water from being pulled in. The other tube should be connected to the growing container top with the next clothespin, putting the end at the medium top, making it flow across the 'soil' line top. The next end must be attached to the outflow spout of the water pump.

Plug the water pump into the timer and it is now time to test out the hydroponic system. Fill the reservoir half way and make sure that the water line is over the tube intake. Plug the timer into an electric socket then set the timer to an 'on' position. There should be a light humming sound from the water pump after couple seconds. Water should start to flow through the tube then out to the reservoir. Check the course of the water in the system to see if there is any leaking occurring and fix it as required.

The hydroponic passive system offers nutrients to the plant by way of a wick or capillary system. Operating in a similar fashion to a kerosene lamp, nutrient solution is drawn by the wick from reservoir, to root system and plant medium. This method is used less than the other and uses mostly peatmoss, sawdust, or sand as growing medium. Moving parts are not involved and it is simple to set up.

It might take a little time to get used to the processes involved in hydroponic gardening, but when it has been learned it can serve as a very successful method of growing any type of plant. Starting with the simpler version, the experience and skills can be developed that are needed to cultivate hydroponically and not have to use costly setups.

Chapter 3 – Mediums For Hydroponics

There are several different mediums as well as numerous mixes. The key thing to think about when selecting a rooting medium is whether or not the chemicals supplied will make the environment hospitable for growing plants. The medium should provide everything a seedling needs, pure water (pH 6.2), weak food, CO_2, low levels light and root oxygen. Below is a list of rooting materials that are more frequently used as well as the advantages and disadvantages for each.

Sand: does not contain a pH buffer but is natural. Check some water that was left in a sample of the sand overnight to see if the selected sand requires pH assistance. Sand drains well but don't hold water too well. It will require a repeated watering schedule. Ensure sand is well washed first so fine particles will not clog the cutting during the taking in of water. Although the nature of sand is temporary it is ideal to root in.

Peat Moss: the pH priority is low as it is organic and the mediums offer the plant a pH buffer. In addition, it retains water adequately in quantities that are not too big. Something similar to Perlite is provided when the quantity is large for increasing drainage. The greatest concern is drowning and food may require added oxygen.

Perlite: this needs pH testing and is synthetic. It aids in correcting to 6.2 and there is no nutrient contained in it so food will have to be supplied. This provides a medium that is very loose which will provide the stalk only minimal support. When necessary, it can be washed out with almost no damage to roots. In fact, it does not hold together. This medium is ideal for root oxygen.

Vermiculite: this is natural but still needs pH testing because of the mineral content. It drains well, providing a little water retention also. Plenty air for oxygenating roots is also available. It is essentially Mica which was superheated to the state of popping into popcorn-like flakes. In the cool state, it has an indefinite amount of micro openings which holds water in each flake.

Rockwool: Although natural, it requires serious pH help. Soak it in a pH of 4.5 for a day from dry prior to using. The issue is that with time, Rockwool will change pH significantly. Water it from the top to allow nutrients to be exchanged in the block. Its drainage is excellent.

Professional Potting Soil: it is generally peat-moss based and it is organic. Generally, the main problems are water saturation and if food is added to the water the plant can be exposed to too many nutrients. These soils hold excess propagation water and drain quite well.

Chapter 4 - Hydroponic Grow Room Atmosphere

The indoor grow room may be arranged almost anywhere, such as a shed, a garage or a spare room. There are only a couple things that need to be considered when you are selecting the most ideal place to be your hydroponic grow room.

The natural atmosphere of the room is an important factor to be considered when the grow room is being selected and set up. We will go into what the air contains that a plant outside will encounter. Growing plants require a continuous source of CO_2 (the gas which they breathe) but unfortunately CO_2 levels found inside often don't have sufficient CO_2 to sustain many plants.

One very important thing to do is to work out the method of producing CO_2 in the levels which are ideal for the kind of plants which will be grown. Generally, plants require approximately 330 parts per million to retain a growing rate that is acceptable and healthy. There are so many different methods of injecting CO_2 into the grow room. CO_2 bottles are available and can be utilized to provide CO_2 by way of a regulator.

There are also CO_2 generators available which burn up propane and generate great levels of CO_2. There are other aspects that need to be considered when dealing with the atmosphere such as negative ions and pest control.

Chapter 5 - Humidity

At some point in your life you may have experienced being in a humid and moist orchid greenhouse. If so, the idea may be in your head that when humidity is at its highest this is ideal for hydroponics. However, this is not the case. The highest vegetable crop humidity range is generally 50% to 80% relative humidity (RH), and 50% is the most ideal. If for any reason it becomes too humid, the plants will not be able to breathe (or transpire) adequately. Air that is very humid is also ideal for fungi and powdery mildew to take hold. When humidity is too high or too low, pollination is difficult.

Get a thermometer-hygrometer and hygrometer combination and hang it in the growing room and check on it daily. You might experience some surprise finding out that the humidity level in the gas-heated or air-conditioned room is quite low.

For raising the garden space humidity, purchase a vaporizer or humidifier that is not too expensive. It is not likely that the humidity on the inside is excessively high, but this can be rectified simply with an oscillating fan (not too high speed) that should be left to run all the 24 hours of the day. This air movement aids in preventing fungus and mold and makes the air exchange better.

Growing hydroponics

If the area you are using is a basement and it's damp, it is recommended that you spend some money on a dehumidifier unit that is portable. This aids in preventing mildew.

If the growing space you selected is a room that is unused or closed off and has no window, for venting the stale air and moisture to the area outside, an exhaust fan like the type that is generally used in bathrooms will be required.

Chapter 6 - Lighting & Other Necessary Tools for Growing Hydroponically

Artificial lighting necessitates using a ballast (this is used for igniting and regulating current to lamp), a reflector or shade (for directing light to the plants), a timer for controlling when lights go on/off) and also the lamp it's self.

Lamp Choice (Enhancing Color Spectrum)

Photosynthesis happens primarily within the spectrum of visible light; 400-700 nanometers wavelength range. In this range, needed most is 650 nanometers (red) 445 nanometers (blue).

High Intensity Discharge (HID) lamps are usually utilized for the flowering or fruiting and vegetative phases because of the high watt per lumens rating. The HID types listed below are used most often:

Metal Halide (MH) lamps generate light mainly in the color blue. This is idyllic for healthy vegetative growth; that is, for example, thicker stems and larger leaves as well as a dense and shorter plant which use light more resourcefully.

High Pressure Sodium (HPS) generates more red color light. This encourages flower budding as well as production and is considered more appropriate for the fruiting or flowering phase.

Lamps with blended light are available to be used throughout, avoiding the requirement of an additional lamp kit (lamp holder, lamp and ballast) for vegetative and flowering phases.

These generate a spectrum of blue and red light that is more balanced.

Fluorescent lamps generate fewer lumens for each watt in comparison to the HID lamps. Therefore, they are used at a limit for plants that require low-medium light strengths, like herbs, seedlings, lettuce, clones, and orchids. They require less energy in use than the HID type lamps as they produce less heat.

Enhancing Light Intensity

If the light is insufficient, there will be sparse foliage being produced as well as inadequate flowering and spindly branches. This may happen because the size and type of lamp as well as lighting duration is not adequate; the distance between the foliage and the lamp is too wide; or other plants are shading the foliage.

Watts (W) are the unit of measure used for lamps. The growing area size will, in part, determine what the necessary wattage is.

The height of the plant should be taken into consideration when the lamp size is being determined as the intensity of light rapidly diminishes in accordance to the increase in the distance away from the lamp.

Shading will be an issue when the plants are too closely positioned to each other. Therefore, it is usually more productive when less is planted than more.

For best usage of the output of the lamp, place the lamp as near as it can be to the plant top without it resulting in burning of the foliage or photo-respiration. Shades that are air-cooled must be used as they allow lamps to be placed a lot closer to the foliage, and this is particularly advantageous for lamps with 1,000 watts or more.

The lamp shades assist in maximizing the level of light that is directed to the plants. The shades require hanging in order that height can be effortlessly adjusted while the plants grow. To ensure safety, mounts are required to be fastened securely to the ceiling.

Plants normally need 18 hours of the day with light when in the vegetative and seedling phase. During fruiting or flowering however, there can be a reduction in duration to only 12 hours. If there is irregularity in the lighting intervals, growth can be thwarted. A timer should therefore be used to aid in ensuring consistency.

Utilizing reflective materials on places such as walls aids in ensuring that light does not get wasted by way of absorption.

Tips for set up and maintenance

Compatibility: Make sure that the lamp and ballast are suited for one another. As an illustration, lamps that are of different kinds (HPS or MH) or varying sizes (Wattages) might need certain ballast. In addition, if an electronic ballast is being used, make sure there is compatibility with the lamp, or else there will be lamp failure of a premature nature and also blackening.

A light meter is essential for deciding whether the light levels are satisfactory in all areas of the "garden" as well as for checking routinely if the lights are working to specification.

Lamps could explode when they are lit while cold or if there are fingerprints on the glass. Ensure they are always wrapped in a clean towel or paper before they are handled. For cleaning the glass of the lamp, rubbing alcohol or window cleaner can be used then allow it to thoroughly dry before use. There should be adequate time between when the lamp is switched off and on again; MH lamps, 20 minutes and HPS, three minutes.

Continuous use will diminish the intensity of the lamp and might also utilize additional power. MH lamps are known to have a shorter working life than HPS. In addition, a magnetic ballast capacitor will weaken with use then the intensity of the light will diminish as a result.

The direction of the lamp will determine whether the lamp is able to be orientated horizontally, vertically etc. Inadequate color or lumen output can result if this rule is not obeyed and the life span of the light can be shortened.

Safety: keep the power devices as well as junctions away from any likely floods of water or spillages, keeping them off the ground will greatly help in this. Ensure electrical cables are rated to manage the current draw of the lights and pump. HID lamps pull a large amount of electricity so safety should be of great importance. A general safety measure includes installing a MCB (miniature circuit breaker) and RCD (residual current device. If a fault develops in the circuit, the power supply will be cut as a result of these safety devices.

Because of the reliability advances that are now being made with digital ballasts, they are now being established as the first choice for more serious gardeners. They are better than magnetic ballasts as they are totally silent, they significantly reduce heat output, and they can be used with an HPS or MH bulb; this makes them the most economical to buy when both types of lamp are to be used.

T5 Fluorescents (T5) are rapidly replacing MH bulbs as first choice for vegetative growth. These fluorescent bulbs of high output operate a lot cooler and this allows them to hang only inches above the plant canopy. This results in a lot denser growth during the vegetative phase.

Here is some detailed information regarding MH and HPS

lighting:

MH- METAL HALIDE

Gardeners know that metal halide bulbs generate between 65 and 115 lumens of light output for each watt of electricity consumed. Light produced from MH bulbs is generated as though resembling a complete summer sun with rich blue from the color spectrum. This enhances rapid vegetative growth as well as stocky and compact plants that have leaf spacing with short internode.

Light is created by metal halide bulbs when an electrical arc is created in an inner clear arc tube which is housed in a clear outer glass vacuum tube. The arc tube contains mercury vapor or other suitable metal vapor. A quite intense heat and light is given off whenever electricity is applied to them. The outside casing may be phosphorus or clear coated.

These bulbs are available in various styles including standard MH and "Super Bulbs"; the super bulbs generate 10-12% additional light but they make use of the same amount of electricity. Although more costly, the super bulbs are more efficient.

Except for the super bulb (1000w), medal halide bulbs are to be replaced approximately every 9500 to 10000 hrs/about 18 months (presuming a cycle of 18 hour per day use). The super bulbs of 100w do not work for long when compared to the others. These should be changed every 6500 hrs/approximately 12 months, and that is if the bulb is run 18 hours each day.

HIGH PRESSURE SODIUM - (HPS)

HPS bulbs are considered to be the most economical bulbs so they are frequently used by the hobby gardener. They fall under the high yellow and red parts on the spectrum and they fall way down on the blue part; this mimics the sun in the fall. Some plants that are cultivated with only HPS lights are able to be grown very leggy and elongated, while not impacted by the issue of light spectrum. This is the frequent choice for plants that generally flower and bud during fall as the light range enhances flower production.

HPS bulbs must be changed after approximately 24 months as brightness and the ability to maintain adequate quality light will slowly be lost from these bulbs

Some people are getting excited about sulfur lighting. For me, I do not use this kind of lighting. Sulfur lighting is expensive in comparison to HID lighting, if you can even get hold of it. This type of lighting is exceptionally bright and energy efficient but there are other problems associated with it including difficulty in obtaining bulbs in the first place.

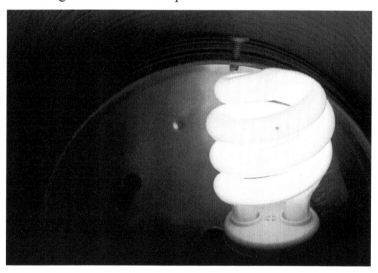

LIGHT MOVERS

Indoor lights are not a perfect sun alternative. Grow lights obviously are not so intense and do not spread over a very large area. Intensity is lost from grow lights very quickly when the space is increased between the plant and the bulb. This indicates that plants are required to be maintained as near to the bulb as is possible for optimum growth. When a light is placed too close to plants, the area of light coverage is lessened and there can also be burning of the plants. Another problem can occur if the plants are kept under stationary light. The plants positioned right under this light will grow noticeably more vigorously when compared to the ones that are a little off to one side. This causes a pyramid effect. Fighting this problem requires the moving around of plants or the light source. It can be challenging or even totally impractical to move the plants, therefore, moving the light in majority of cases is the sole option.

The two types of light movers are circular and linear. Circular movers change around 2-3 lights in a circular fashion and are created for usage in a round or square garden. The linear movers make the light move back and forth along a straight line and operate adequately in gardens that are rectangular in shape.

The advantages of light movers include: the lights can be brought nearer to the plants without worries about burning them; they provide additional light coverage (coverage can be increased by 25-30%); they give the garden more adequate light distribution; transmit light to plants from several angles rather than only one as would be the case with a stationary light.

Chapter 7 - Nutrients

Gardeners may optimize growing conditions when they give the crops the correct strength and formula of nutrients as they grow. Purchase a hydroponic nutrient that is formulated for the growing medium that you use; there are some fertilizers that are mixed particularly for mixes of soilless potting, but they do not work properly for crops that grow in Rockwool.

The fertilizer called green growth should be used until the light hours are shortened and then changed to flowering or food for crop production.

It is essential to consider increasing the strength of the food when the light levels are intense and the ideal air movement is set up in the garden. Growing conditions should first be evaluated. If all is going great and the plants are in an active growth period, the food strength should be gradually increased while carefully examining the crops for stress symptoms. The stage of green growth is short (normally only 10-14 days) so there will not be a lot of time available to increase the strength of the food while in this stage.

In the period of 'transition' (after the day length is shortened and before flowers start showing), there is no need for excessive growth, and many gardeners reduce the fertilizer strength until there is a showing of flowers on the plants.

As soon as the plants begin to produce flowers, they now are entering an active growth period, and it can prove to be helpful if the nutrient strength is increased. This should be done gradually and carefully. Food strength should be increased by approximately 200 PPM and crops should be closely watched to ensure that they can adjust to the new, stronger, mix strength. When a few days have passed, if all is proceeding well, the nutrient strength should be increased again by the same amount. When the plants are carefully watched how they react to the increased level, the growers can quickly learn what the correct food strength is for their garden and their plants.

Chapter 8 – Kelp

Kelp is one of the various large brown seaweeds which grow underwater as well as on shores with a lot of rocks. They are located worldwide in cold water.

There are several forms and sizes of kelp. One of them, giant kelp, can have several dozens of branches, and there are several hundreds of leaves on each branch. Giant kelp can span more than 200ft in length; it can produce a complete kelp forest. There are other kelp that have one branch only and can be less than 3ft in length. With all of them, it is difficult to differentiate the leaves from the stems.

The role that kelp plays in agriculture goes back several thousand years and has become a vital aspect of farming on the coast. It has been proven that kelp, next to excellent fertilizer, is a very highly efficient additive.

The most important kelp is Ascophyllum Nodosum which is cultivated in the cold Atlantic Ocean waters. There are several kelp which have excellent benefits in agriculture but this specific one is the best of the best.

The methods for harvesting ascophyllum include collecting it from shores that are full of rocks or using some kind of seine or dredge to capture it. Fresh water is then used to wash it to get rid of any extra sea salt and pollutants. It is then dried and powdered. It is essential that it is harvested at the right time to make sure that the levels of cytokinin (growth hormones in charge of plant cell division) are at the optimized peak. There are more than 70 minerals as well as trace elements, vitamins, growth hormones, proteins and enzymes in kelp.

Research has shown that the kelp itself or the contents is able to speed up growth, increase flowering and fruiting, help frost and drought resistance, fight insects and disease. One important thing to note about kelp benefits and how they operate is that every trace element and mineral that carbohydrate mannitol helps to chelate or allow particular minerals to be available, work to support the natural immune system of the plant.

The next essential, and maybe the most vital, aspect of kelp: growth hormones. There are more than enough cytokinins, gibberellins and auxins. Every growth hormone plays a role in the way a plant functions. They are more commonly known as growth regulators. There are very high levels of cytokinin hormone in kelp. These are in charge of cell division, its enlargement, variation of cells, chloroplasts development and also aging delay.

A lot of ways are available to utilize kelp and foliar spraying is considered the most effective one. For instance, if buds start appearing on your peas and tomatoes, kelp can be applied to encourage additional buds. If more root growth is required, then it should be applied to the area of the root after transplanting.

The types and benefits of kelp are many and varied. Granular kelp, for example, is frequently combined with some fertilizers and the cytokinins that they contain are not as high in comparison to liquid concentrate. If you desire to supplement the current fertilizer regime that you have you would maybe need powered kelp added. If you are, however, attempting to encourage more budding or flowering sites then a Growth Plus or Growth Max, which is a concentrated kelp liquid, product can be used.

The most successful method of applying the kelp is foliar spraying, because leaves are a maximum of 7 times more efficient in digesting nutrients when compared to methods involving the root system. When using this type of spraying, it is recommended that it is applied in the morning at an early time when there is more action from the plant and stomata are fully opened. Spraying just before it rains is not advised and water of high quality should be used (6.0 pH).

In summary, kelp is able to assist in germinating seeds quicker; improve cuttings takings; boost rooting; develop immunity; give additional flavor and color; offer an extended shelf life; generate more and also larger flowers and buds; fight against nutrient deficiencies; and battle against diseases and insects. Kelp is really Mother Nature's gift to gardener of today.

Chapter 9 - Pests

The processes of controlling insects that are pests with chemical sprays have resulted in a high level of concern for gardeners as well as consumers. The concerns are in regards to the environment, children's health and well as that of pets and also for gardeners who are dispensing these chemicals or individuals who have to work with these plants when they have the spray on them. Regrettably, several of the chemicals are known as 'non-selective'; this means they do not only destroy the pests that are being targeted but also kill a whole load of insects that are good as well.

The greatest concern today is the issue of toxic products being used on produce which is cultivated for humans to consume. As such, many indoor gardeners are now using insect control measures that are beneficial while managing their problem with pests.

Beneficial insects help the gardener when they kill (often eating) insect pests and remove the requirement for toxic chemical use. These insects usually get rid of the pests in one way or the other: parasitize or are predators of these pests.

The insects that are beneficially parasitic actually rely on the pest insects to survive as they have to lay eggs on or in them. The newborn beneficial insects feed on the body of the pest and kill the 'host'.

The beneficial predator insects are the ones which actually make a meal of the insect pest. Therefore, they depend on these pests for survival.

A beneficial insect that is highly effective is called a parasitic wasp. They generally lay eggs in a particular pest at an early stage of the pest's life (the pupal, larval or egg stage). The larvae grow in the pest, kill it and the wasps then emerge to seek another host for laying their eggs; the cycle continues.

To keep beneficial insects in greenhouses, it is required that they are supplied with water and food, the life essentials. In general, the majority of parasitic wasps prefer nectar which is the sweet fluid that flowers secrete (a solution of sugar and water may suffice as a substitute). When they can survive, their life span is extended and they are able to look for more pest insects in which to lay eggs. This gets rid of more of these unwanted insects and also creates biological control for future generations.

Bear in mind that when the wasp is small, the need will be greater for plants that have small flowers. This will be easier for the wasp to get the nectar. Dill is an ideal plant for the wasps. It grows tall but has a whole lot of small flowers that are clustered together making the nectar easy for the small wasps to group around. Other great plants are coriander, fennel, parsley and caraway. The parasitic wasps are known to go to small flowers for their nectar source, but predator insects are proven to also visit the flowers to have a meal of pollen, particularly lacewing and adult as well as juvenile ladybugs.

One other common beneficial insect which operates by parasitizing a host is beneficial nematode. This insect travels through a medium and finding larvae of insects by picking up a little temperature increase or methane gas release. When they have located their 'host', this nematode goes into its body by journeying through natural openings like the mouth. When they are inside this host, symbiotic bacteria are released by them which result in paralyzing their hosts and killing them in 24 to 48 hours. These nematodes then feed on this bacteria as well as the decayed tissue of the host. Where there is reproduction the number grows until there is no more space to hold all of them and they are required to find new hosts.

Larval nematodes are able to survive outwith a host for up to twelve months if the temperature and moisture levels are favorable and remain that way.

A moist and dark environment is required by the nematodes. If the soil temperatures remain consistent for growing indoors, you do not have to be concerned about the hibernating of nematodes. Only when there is a temperature drop in the winter time, the nematodes will go further down in the soil and start hibernating. When the temperature starts to rise in spring, they will come nearer the surface of the soil. Unfortunately, the return of these nematodes generally takes longer than that of the pests that reside in the soil. Therefore, pest control that is most effective re-introduces the beneficial nematodes in the early part of spring each year or for every time that there is a change in the growing medium.

There are more than 250 varying species of soil pests being controlled by beneficial nematodes. These species include some very damaging ones such as wire worms, weevils (especially harmful to new plants), pill bugs, sow bugs, earwigs, grubs and fungus gnats. Most of the pests from the soil can be managed with frequent application of the beneficial nematodes and this can be done in the fall or spring or any time there is an alteration in growing medium.

Mites are included in the predator pests. The spider mite with two spots is usually a great concern for indoor growers. Their life span is 15 days; however, they can accomplish a lot of damage in that short span of life. In addition 50 to 100 eggs can be laid by the female before it dies. Every stage of the spider mite's development is cause for concern regarding plant damage. This is because the mite feeds on the plant cells. There will be a yellowing of the cells which results in the leaf speckling. Where the damage is greater, there will be a noticeable and complete yellowing of the leaf and it will die.

If you think that there might be spider mites, you can search for them where they usually dwell: the plant leaves undersides. When webbing is noticed on the plant, it indicates that the mites have gotten to the levels of infestation.

Incredibly though, a highly effective control of these spider mites is known to be a predatory insect of their kind, known as Phytoseiulus Persimilis. This mite is shaped like a pear and has long legs. They can be confused at times with the summer mites which change to an orange color whenever they hibernate.

This adult predator mite can eat from 5 to 20 prey, mites or eggs, each day. The reason they are this effective against the pest mites is the fact that they can reproduce more rapidly at temperatures that are over 82°F (28°C) when compared to the spider mite.

They also feed on every state of the spider mite pests. However, the Persimilis require humidity levels that are high (over 60%) which also have effects on spider mites to cause a reduction in the laying of eggs.

Since these mites can be efficient dispersers and hunters, they can result in the elimination of the prey, which really is very desirable where there can be no or just a little damage by these pests tolerated, like in ornamental plants.

Eventually, the Persimilis will use up the food supply they have and starve. As a result, it should be reintroduced whenever there is a new infestation of spider mite.

The Feltiella Acarisuga is one other great predatory insect for controlling the spider mite. This insect is approximately 1 ½ inches in length and has a brown-pinkish color. Eggs will be laid by the female Feltiella inside the colonies of the spider mites and immediately when the hatching of young larvae occurs, they start to feast on the eggs of the spider mite.

Young larvae mainly feed on these eggs and older larvae will feed on the spider mite at all its life stages. The Feltiella lifespan from egg stage to adult is generally 10 to 15 days and about 12 to 14 eggs will be laid by them. Like the Persimilis, when the food supply has been exhausted, they will starve and therefore should be introduced again whenever there are new infestations.

Some of the beneficial predators that are best to use are those that will remain in the garden when they are released, particularly those that do not have their wings developed yet.

The ladybug and lacewing larvae are voracious eaters of aphids as, in essence, these are teenagers that have huge appetites, not sexually active as yet, and completely focused on the eating task. They usually remain and 'clean' the area a lot better because they are able only to crawl to go in search of what they will eat, and they have not developed wings to fly to go look for mates yet. Aphids will be eaten by the adult size ladybug but as the lacewing matures, they start to feed on pollen only.

For gardeners, a mix of pest control (predator and parasite) for controlling the problem is the most ideal recommendation. A great example is the aphid control; allow adult ladybugs to consume adult aphids and also lay their eggs in the aphid egg colony, but also utilize the Aphidius Colemani, which is a type of parasitic wasp, for controlling the larvae and eggs.

Most importantly to bear in mind when making use of beneficial insects is to avoid using pesticides as well because they will often kill the beneficial insects along with the pests.

Chapter 10 - Ebb & Flow

The Ebb and Flow system utilizes two 5-gallon buckets or containers or anything that is equivalent. The growing medium is filled in one of them and nutrient solution is in the other.

The bucket with the nutrient solution is lifted to water the plants. This causes a flow of the solution to the bucket that has the growing medium and the plants. For draining, just lower the bucket with the nutrient and natural gravity will drain solution back to the reservoir.

Materials Required

- **Buckets:** Two 5-gallon or plastic water tight container that is equivalent. Ensure that there are no leaks in the buckets.

- **Growing medium:** Experts prefer direct Perlite or the

Perlite/Vermiculite combination for this arrangement. However, there is a wide range of growing media that are also acceptable.

- **Flexible vinyl tubing:** A length of ½ inch diameter flexible tubing is required that is sufficiently long to accommodate the movement of the buckets; 4-5 inches is generally adequate. There is also a requirement for flexible tubing of the same length to join the air stone with the air pump.

- **Fiberglass window screen:** A small quantity of window (12-inch x 12-inch) fiberglass screen.

- **Air stone and air pump:** An air pump as well as air stone is required for oxygenating the nutrient solution. A standard air pump that is designed for use with an aquarium is fine.

- **Grommets:** 2 x ½ -inch.

- **Straight barbed connectors:** 2 x ½ -inch.

- **Gravel:** Sufficient gravel is required to cover the bottom of the growing container to a depth of about 2 to 3-inches.

  Use relatively coarse gravel of ¾ -inch to 1-inch diameter. Please note that a five-gallon bucket requires approximately 1-gallon of gravel to get to this level.

- **Hydroponic fertilizer:** one that is of good quality is required. The fertilizers that are designed for use in soil do not have the necessary micro-nutrients.

- **pH Test Kit:** It is required that you check and then adjust the nutrient solution pH.

System Assembly

Make two holes in one of the plastic buckets (clean) that are about ½ -inch above the bottom then insert grommets.

Put in ½ inch barbed connectors (straight) into grommets and join both ends of the ½ inch tubing to the connectors.

Put gravel in the bottom of one bucket. This will serve as the planter while the next one is the reservoir.

Put the fiberglass over the gravel top. Fold any leftover over or use scissors to trim it. The role of the fiberglass is as a filter for keeping growing medium in its place, so the screen should be fitted a near to the bucket sides as possible. The fit does not have to be perfect but when the screen is more snugly fitted, this will reduce the likelihood of growing medium getting washed down into the reservoir when the system is drained in the Ebb cycle. If there is too much of the growing medium going through the screen, this may clog up the drain or fill tubes.

The growing medium should now be added to the bucket. Presoak and/or wash the growing medium prior to adding it to the system, determined by the kind of medium that is being used.

Plant the seedlings, seeds or rooted cuttings in the medium. Experts recommend that the seeds are started separately and seedlings added to the system.

Feeding and Care Instructions

Place the planter on the raised platform and allow the reservoir to remain in the lowered position. If there is nothing already in place as a platform, one can be made quite easily. Place two regular masonry blocks on their ends and put a board that is sufficiently large to hold the two buckets on top of it.

Fill up the reservoir with some water and combine the available nutrient solution according to the instructions on the packet. Take a look at the nutrient solution pH and make adjustments in accordance with what you find. The pH value that is required will be different and is determined by what is required for the plant as well as the type of growing medium. Place a lid that is loose fitting on the reservoir to cover it and keep out debris but not air-tight. The nutrient solution should be aerated by using an air stone and an air pump to prevent it from becoming stagnated.

For feeding and watering your plants, you should just lift up the reservoir container and place it beside the planter bucket on the platform. Give it a few minutes before lowering the reservoir to its original place. It is important to keep in mind that there are 40 pounds wight in a full 5-gallon bucket. If you are not able to lift up that much, it is advised that you make smaller quantities of the nutrient solution.

The frequency of doing a watering cycle will be determined by one or more of many variables; weather conditions, types and size of the plants, the kind of growing medium, among others. It can become somewhat of a guessing situation until you get used to it. However, it is very hard to water the plants too much so if you are in doubt, still do it!

Check out the nutrient solution pH every two days or so and make adjustments if required.

When 50% of this nutrient solution has been used up by the plants, you can go ahead and add only water to bring the level back up. Ensure that you do not put in more fertilizer or a build-up of nutrient may occur and that is likely to damage the plants. If necessary, have another look at the pH and make any necessary adjustments.

When this nutrient solution is down to the halfway mark again, the solution now needs to be changed and this is done by allowing the reservoir to drain and mix another fresh batch. The used up nutrient solution can be used on house plants as well as other vegetation.

About The Author

Allen Dunn has heard of and tried numerous things in his lifetime and he could not pass up the opportunity to try out the hydroponics way of gardening. He found that it was ideal for the types of plants he wants to grow and also that not only is it simple and easy to do, it saved him a lot of money in the long run.

His extensive research brought him useful information regarding how you can do your own hydroponics gardening, the different mediums that are used, the correct temperature for this type of gardening, and even the types of insects that can harm or help the gardening process.

Dunn also want to share with readers what he found out about lighting and other essential equipment for hydroponics gardening. He has documented his knowledge and experience in how to control the harmful pests as well as the nutrient that is very vital in this type of growing system.

Allen Dunn has shared the information in this book in such a manner that persons who are considering this or those who are hearing about it for the first time will find out how simple and ideal it is to choose the hydroponics method of gardening.

Made in the USA
Lexington, KY
27 August 2014